The Fourteen
Home Selling Secrets
The Mistakes Everyone Makes

By Bob Easter
President, Easter and Easter, Inc.

ISBN: 1-885257-01-5

This book is designed to provide accurate and authoritative information with regard to the subject matter covered. It is sold with the
understanding that the publisher is not engaged in rendering legal,
accounting, or other professional advice. If legal advice or other
expert assistance is required, the services of a competent professional
person should be sought. Real estate practices and laws differ from
state to state. Legal questions should be addressed by an attorney.

About Bob Easter

Bob Easter has been in the real estate business longer than most people have been in their first homes.

While some of his close friends call him a "visionary" and a "leading edge businessman," few people know just how much experience and expertise he has.

To begin, Bob Easter is President and owner of the Easter and Easter real estate office in Austin, Texas, and publisher of the *Express*, his own popular real estate newspaper for the Austin area. He has been operating one of the top ten real estate offices in Austin for more than twelve years now.

Bob is a leading advocate for protecting consumer rights. He originated the first seller's disclosure form to be used in the Austin real estate market in 1986. Now that such disclosures are required by Texas law, Bob's form is currently being requested throughout Texas - and is even drawing national attention - because of its clarity, ease of use and depth of questions.

But that's not all. He is the past president of the Texas Circulation Management Association and the North West Area Chamber of Commerce as well as past Board Director of the Austin Chamber of Commerce. He's also an inventor holding a U.S. Patent, a TV producer of a real estate show and the author of an earlier book entitled *The Numbers Game*, about his experience in newspaper circulation.

This busy man has also won numerous awards, including winning first place twice for the Best Newspaper Promotion, winning first place **five** times from the International Circulation Management Association and winning first place awards ten times from the Texas Circulation Management Association.

But hold on! There's still more to Bob Easter. As a speaker, he has addressed the American Press Institute at Columbia University, Southern Newspaper Publishers Association, Austin Chamber of Commerce, Austin American-Statesman and The American Press Institute in Reston, Virginia, among many others.

As a consultant he has worked with a wide range of organizations and publications. Bob and his wife, Carolyn, have a combined family of five adult children and two grandchildren.

This is Bob Easter, a positive thinking man dedicated to family, friends, and helping everyday people buy and sell the homes of their dreams in fun and profitable ways. He wrote this book out of his commitment to help others benefit from his enormous experience in real estate.

Thank you, Bob Easter!

By Joe Vitale

*"The 14 Home Selling Secrets, The Mistakes Everyone
Makes the home selling process easy to understand.
This book is full of money saving secrets. Order this
book today!"*
- Sonny Block
America's Financial Consumer Advocate,
Author, and Nationally Syndicated Talk Show Host

*"Bob Easter's book The 14 Home Selling Secrets, The
Mistakes Everyone Makes is a masterpiece! It contains
a gold mine of the latest and greatest information for
home sellers. It will save you valuable time, energy and
money."*
- Anne Boe
Speaker/Author,
Is Your Net Working and Net Working Success

*"When I want or need help, I want help from an experi-
enced professional! Bob Easter is one of those people...
Not only do I know him, but I trust him. His book is
step-by-step advice from a 'pro'. Anybody who buys
this book, reads this book and follows Bob's advice will
get both answers and encouragement."*
- Lewis R. Timberlake
Author, Lecturer, Consultant

"Bob Easter is an advocate for consumer rights who is trying to help the average person win in today's 'sue happy' world. His new hardcover book, titled The 14 Home Selling Secrets, The Mistakes Everyone Makes is an easy to understand resource designed to help anyone safely, enjoyably and profitably sell their own home."

\- Mark Weisser
Assistant Editor, DBA Magazine
Houston, Texas

"An easy to read manual that spares readers real estate jargon."

\- Amy Smith
Feature Writer, Austin Business Journal

"Easter's book is direct and honest. The 14 Home Selling Secrets, The Mistakes Everyone Makes is designed to make the home selling journey a smooth one. It's an inexpensive ounce of prevention."

\- Greg Stiles
Arcadia News
Phoenix , Arizona

Acknowledgements

No author is successful without wonderful friends to encourage and support the dream of putting into words what is felt in one's heart. This book has become a reality because a group of friends were able to generously give much needed suggestions and help. I would like to thank my dear friend, Mark Victor Hansen, who was always positive that my experiences in real estate would be valuable to anyone who wanted to sell their home. Mark also suggested that Ann Fisher would have the skills to make the words flow with the greatest of ease. Thanks, Ann, for all your editorial help.

Becky Putnam has been an angel in disguise, doing the typing corrections and re-typing during all of the makeovers. Dawn Callihan put the final touches on the final drafts.

Kudos to Gary Selman who introduced me to Joe Vitale. Joe's enthusiasm about self-publishing and his endless suggestions helped me to make this book a reality.

No person or project is ever successful without support from family. To my children, and to my wife and soul mate, Carolyn, thank you for all your patience and love.

Foreword

Real Estate is the business that has and will continue to create more wealth than any other industry. It is reported that 97% of the world's millionaires have their vast assets tied up financing real estate - personally and commercially.

If you want an insider's idea of how the real estate industry works, this is it. Learn how you can work it from the inside-out and experience great earnings with relative safety and security. The "Fourteen Home Selling Secrets" outlined in this book are easy to follow and understand.

Bob Easter and I have been friends for many years. He is Mr. Integrity - personified. He has experienced all the ups and downs, thrills and chills that real estate has to offer - as an owner of real estate, salesman and real estate broker. He is a student, scholar, investor and counselor to many in his city of Austin - best and richest people. He is respected, admired, appreciated and loved by all of us who know him. Formerly, he was a successful newspaper executive, speaker and author. Now he wants to share his insider knowledge, wisdom and facts. You will learn what it takes to make his industry more user friendly. He provides a steady course to guide you through the home selling process by giving you the inside tips and mistakes that everyone makes when they plan to sell real estate.

Bob is a great, caring man with a gigantic loving heart who wants to share from his wisdom and abundance of experience.

     I am thankful he wrote this book. After reading it, I believe you will be too.

> *Mark Victor Hansen*
> Co-Author: Chicken Soup
> for the Soul
> Author: Dare to Win
> Newport Beach, CA

CONTENTS

INTRODUCTION

Back in the 1950's and 60's, when my brother and I were growing up, I watched my single parent mother support her family by selling residential real estate. She had a never-give-up attitude, and it was this indomitable spirit of hers which got us through some very tough times. But nothing in my childhood or my career as owner of a Top 10 real estate firm in Austin, Texas, prepared me for the devastating collapse—from 1985 to 1991—of the entire real estate market. However, if it weren't for my early economic hardships and those lessons learned from a remarkable mother, I would never have been prepared at all to grow and prosper during this downward real estate spiral.

Bankruptcy, foreclosures, empty homes, vacant apartments and buildings were part of our everyday life for almost six years. For me, it was a painful sight--the vacated and all too abundant shells were the only remaining skeletons of what were once peoples' hopes and dreams. Only a short time earlier, the owners and tenants called these places home, filling them with laughter, plans, goals, memories and, above all, families. This was the hardest thing to deal with during those six years -- we were the bearer of bad news to thousands of families. Some were luckier than others, but even today, I can still hear their hurt and see the pain and worry on their faces when they understood that they were in danger of losing their home.

The single biggest issue that we had to deal with was the unfair policies of mortgage lenders who established rules that made it impossible for honest, hard-working homeowners to refinance their loan for the full principal balance at a lower interest rate. Many of these homeowners were already paying 11, 12 and 13% interest and then, unfortunately, were foreclosed upon with a higher principal balance than their home was worth! On top of that came additional attorneys' fees, court costs and the inventory holding cost of the property. All this, along with necessary repairs and time spent on the market for resell at a much lower price, eventually added more emotional and financial grief to the already existing economic problems of the homeowner.

Although we were successful in negotiating with some lenders, this was the exception rather than the rule. By and large, most mortgage companies took a hard line toward homeowners. I believe it was due to the guaranteed private mortgage insurance fund, along with government-backed programs which enabled the lender to recoup the losses after foreclosure.

When I sat down to write this book, my purpose was clear: I wanted to help people avoid making the kind of mistakes that could lead to what I've just described above, and which hundreds of thousands of homeowners in Texas, and many other states, refused to hear before it was too late. I want to help you understand the necessity and importance of listening to a professional in order to escape the pitfalls and costly mistakes that will inevitably occur--I've seen it happen too many times--and I know that with the proper advice and preparation, it doesn't have to be this way.

Regardless of your belief system about the current real estate market in your area or how you arrived at your present position of thinking, the mistakes I've detailed in this book are those that will prevent you from being able to sell your home today—or at any time in the future. That's because it's not usually just one mistake that's involved, but rather a series of errors in judgment which have carried over from a boom market--when any home would sell quickly and for the asking price--to what we are faced with today: a slow or down market, and in many areas of the country, a seriously declining one. Even when a market is active and improving, errors in judgment by the home-owners occur on a regular basis.

Trying to sell your home in any type of market, declining, stable or improving, can lead to:

1) a major hassle, costing you thousands of dollars if your home does not sell,

2) becoming psychologically/emotionally depressed because your home has been on the market without receiving an offer from a potential buyer and,

3) costing you time and inconvenience by having to show the home over an extended period of time without achieving results.

There's a lot at stake here: time, money, convenience, peace of mind. Thus, more than ever before, it is time to learn new lessons in order to insure the success of your goal. A change in your thinking and approach is going to be necessary. You must also be able to put yourself in the buyer's shoes--to understand the current market from their point of view--and to know how many homes are readily available in the marketplace at any given time. Your competition includes resell and new homes.

I hope that you will take advantage of the experience that I have accumulated over the twelve years of operating a successful real estate business, with five of those years during the worst declining market our city has ever experienced. I believe that my suggestions, insights and tips are going to spare you from making the costly mistakes you'll be reading about in the following chapters.

The only good real estate transaction I know is the one that is closed and funded. Regardless of the current market conditions or whether or not you use the services of a real estate agent, I want to enable you to make the selling of your home a fun and profitable experience. Having a winning game plan is what this book is all about and is the spirit in which I wrote it. Use it well, be guided by it, and I know it will work for you.

CHAPTER ONE

Taking Action

*"The instinct of ownership is
fundamental in man's nature."*
—William James

Not long ago, a client asked me a question that brought me up short. "Bob," he said, "if you are telling me to sell in this market, what and why are you telling buyers to purchase real estate when the prices are so unstable?" I really hadn't thought that one through before and his inquiry was unsettling. Our real estate company had earned quite a reputation for being consumer friendly. But was my advice based on sound reasoning? How could both parties gain?

In a changing market—one that is going up or down in prices—both parties attempt to put themselves in an advantageous financial position where they can profit, break even or at least prevent as much loss as possible. But the fact is, regardless of market conditions, not all parties in a real estate transaction will benefit. Sometimes there are economic losses. (Ask any investor about the 1985-86 tax laws passed by Congress and you will understand how careless our federal government can be with the taxpayers' economic future.) We've always explained the market to our customers by pointing out that in a normal year, less than five to ten percent of the residential homes are sold and that each homeowner's situation is different.

They enter the market at different times and sell their property for different reasons, i.e., some are transferred, some die, others move up to a larger home while others are downsizing.

The hardest hit of all these customers were the ones who had purchased at the peak of the boom in 1984-85; however, they made up less than five percent of our total housing market. Since no market jumps overnight, our boom time was building up over a six-year period. It's necessary for homeowners to understand that their perception of the market plays an important role in how fast a recovery will take place.

We were honest with owners and buyers. Some homeowners just couldn't sell. A term I grew to dislike was "they are buried" which meant the seller would be forced to wait out the recovery period, rent the property and make up a monthly negative cash flow, or walk away and allow foreclosure. Our job was to determine the cost of selling during this time, and there were many instances when we simply advised the homeowners to wait.

When a property changes ownership, the new cost of purchasing that property establishes the new market value. While it was true that some sellers actually did lose their hard equity in the property, most sellers lost "appreciated" equity. This is the equity that builds up in a property from the time of purchase to the time of sale. Some people like to refer to it as "funny money," which means you can't touch it, see it or take it with you. If your house is appreciating in value, then so are most of your neighbors' homes. So if you take your appreciated equity and purchase a more expensive home, the money disappears. If values are going down, the appreciated equity shrinks.

The fact is most buyers know what the market is doing at any given time, so they bargain for the very best deal. The buyer's purchase price for a home may be the new current market value, and at the same time, the seller may have lost their appreciated equity but not all of their actual equity. Because the owners purchased the home in 1985 for $150,000, the price rose until 1990 when it topped out at $190,000. While the owner may have sold in 1993 for $150,000, the perceived loss by that seller was $40,000.

It's for this reason that I often counsel people that home ownership is not intended to be a profit-driven purpose. Trying to recover all of your equity really doesn't make sense--after all, you wouldn't ask a landlord to give you back all the rent you paid over a lease term. Sometimes we lose sight of the fact that it costs something to live in a home or a rental unit.

All of which leads me to, once again, remind you that everything you will read in the next thirteen chapters is going to help you better understand the market, the attitudes of buyers and sellers, the misperceptions and mistakes that I want to prevent you from making when selling your home—whether it's today, tomorrow or in the future.

CHAPTER TWO

Over Pricing Your Home

Allowing emotion or pride to keep you from admitting that the perceived value of your home has anything to do with what it is worth in today's market.

Your Home Is Worth Less Than You Think

Home ownership has a very personal bearing on how we perceive, think and feel about many aspects of our lives. Since time immemorial our home has been our fortress, our castle keeping us away from danger and protecting us from the elements. It is where we can feel safe, a refuge from the outside world. Our home is a special place that identifies our lifestyle and reflects our taste, creativity, sense of responsibility, personal habits and attitudes. It tells the whole world what we care about and who we are.

Our memories of past events, special holidays, births and deaths, family marriages and even divorce, become part of the fabric we weave when placing a value on our home, one that usually tends to cloud our judgment when we plan to sell. Our perception of value really doesn't reflect what the market is doing at that particular time. Buyers buy by comparing prices and properties on the market today. Sellers attempt to sell based on emotions and the investment they have made in the property both in terms of money and work. Selling memories, emotions or improvements usually fails. Therefore our pride and many other personal feelings keep us off center enough to confuse our picture of real estate reality, especially when we recall the **"boom"** market prices and how we could have sold our property during the good years for a much higher price. Looking back at the past market and past mistakes is an unpleasant regret that permeates our present thinking more than we realize and it keeps us from making the right decision *now*. Regardless of whether the market is declining or improving, pride can cost us real money, especially when we are afraid to admit our mistakes.

Who Establishes Value?

Value of property is basically determined by what a willing buyer is prepared to pay for that property. The buyer may not appreciate your home as much as you do or be willing to understand the care and attention you have given it all these years, and he or she certainly does not place any value on the memories you treasure and the hours of labor spent on improving and maintaining it.

No one should ever try to put a price tag on what or how the present owner values the property. Years of love, sweat and tears cannot be replaced or used as a factor to determine value. That is exactly the reason why banks, mortgage companies and lenders require that an independent appraiser look at the property and establish a fair market value.

Buyers Are Looking For Bargains, Not Your Perceived Value

That's good, because you now have the opportunity to position your home as a bargain!

One of the most difficult issues that a Real Estate Agent/Broker faces when dealing with a homeowner is how to communicate effectively about the emotional issues involved. I have seen owners lose a sale over a mere $200! This is because they were negotiating a contract with the prospective buyer from a point of pride. It's the sort of thing that can cost the homeowner several thousand dollars six months down the line.

To help you understand how important it is to remain flexible during negotiations, let's use this example: Let's say that the market in your area has fallen 12% since last year. You list your home for $150,000 which is what the current market analysis, sometimes referred to as Competitive Market Analysis (CMA) or Broker Price Opinion (BPO), by several Real Estate Agent/Brokers estimates your home to be worth today. **Remember, a market analysis is not an official appraisal unless the real estate laws in your state recognize the market analysis as an appraisal.**

You list your home for sale and after 45 days you receive an offer of $145,000. The buyer is willing to close in the next 45 days. Your immediate reaction is hostile because you believe the offer is too low. So you counter the buyer to $148,000, telling the Real Estate Agent/ Broker that is your bottom line—take it or leave it. The buyer counters the offer to $146,500 and declares that is his final offer. You refuse to negotiate again because you believe the value of the home is still worth $150,000, and you don't intend to "give" your home away. The buyer walks away, and later you find out that he has purchased another home down the street.

Why was it so easy for you to make the mistake of allowing emotion or pride to keep you from accepting what the true value of your home is in today's market? Let's take the problem apart.

1) Current market conditions: Declining --
   Depreciation: 12% annually
2) Listed Price: $150,000
3) Monthly decrease in value: 1% per month
4) Offer made: 45 days after listing signed
5) Closing date of contract: 45 days from offer
6) Total time on market: 90 days — 45 days on market, 45 days to closing
7) Estimated new value on day of closing: $145,500 -- Using 1% depreciation per month = 12% per year.
8) Buyer's final offer: $146,500

The buyer actually made a $1,000 better offer than the home was worth. Thus, sticking with the "perceived" value of your home will cost you money if you fail to factor in declining market conditions and allow your emotions or pride to set prices.

Sometimes a seller will demand a higher listed price even after they have seen evidence of a declining market in their area. In a later chapter we will discuss how this position can cause you a great deal of stress and possibly keep your home from ever selling.

Don't Blame The Appraiser

Many sellers simply do not understand that even if they secure an acceptable offer on their property from a willing buyer, the home must still be appraised. Strict new federal regulations and appraisal guidelines sometimes make it difficult for the appraiser to justify the sale price of the home. If that happens, it is imperative to take immediate action to see if you can afford to accept the new appraised price. Unfortunately, most sellers I've seen in this situation have an immediate negative reaction and start blaming the appraiser or Real Estate Agent/Broker. The fact is that neither the Real Estate Agent/Broker or appraiser determine the market. **Buyers determine what they are willing to pay for a home.** The appraisal reflects the actual facts of what other buyers were willing to pay for similar homes in your neighborhood.

A Note of Caution: Because the appraisal process is based on historical information, the appraiser is normally too low in a rising market and too high in a declining market.

Your real estate agent should be able to offer positive steps that can be taken if the appraiser has overlooked important information. If your agent is not sure what to do or if you do not have an agent, write for our publication: Appraiser Tips c/o Easter & Easter/Better Homes and Gardens, 4212 Lostridge Drive, #200, Austin, Texas, 78731. See order coupon in back of book.

In a Static or Improving Market Buyers Are Still Looking For The Best Value

Just as in a declining market, buyers are looking for the best home for the least amount of money.

All homeowners should ask themselves the question: "What factors would motivate me to purchase if I were buying a home in a static or improving economy?" The answer is simple, especially if the choice is between two similar homes in terms of neighborhood, location and amenities. While the buyer is looking for or concentrating on value, they will also base part of their reason for purchase on emotion.

When you are negotiating an offer on your property, carefully read the special conditions of your contract wherein the buyer asks for the curtains in the children's room, or the playscape, or the chandelier in the dining room to convey with the property. These are clear signals. The buyer is telling you that your home is equal to other homes, but these additional items will make this buyer ready to purchase your home today.

Again, I want to caution you about losing a sale over emotional items. While the playscape is a treasured part of your home today, your children may be grown and long gone before another buyer shows up! Even in a boom market some homes never sell. Listings expire or property is taken off the market in the best of times. Therefore, remember that the buyer must perceive value before becoming emotionally involved. Once their emotions enter into the process, they usually tell you what key issues are important to them for the deal to work. **The secret is to keep the emotional items in the contract in order for the buyer to stay hooked.** Conveying a small item with the property is often an inducement to buy and is much better than keeping the home on the market.

Home Prices Are Going Up, So Why Should I Be Motivated to Take Less Than I Want For My Home?

Our memories are shortlived, especially if we recall the last real estate boom or bust. In a declining market, the longer you have your home up for sale, the more you lose. When a market is improving, the longer you wait for a sale, the higher the cost of your new home. Selling a home also requires emotional and physical energy, and it can be draining for the whole family. The sooner you sell, the better the future looks.

A contract and closing on your old home finishes the chapter and makes you ready for the future. Sign the contract and close quickly in a boom market to avoid your new home costing even more. Note: If prices are increasing 1% per month, then a $100,000 home will increase by $1,000 in thirty days. When you are negotiating for a new home in a market where prices are escalating, it is to your advantage to extend the closing date as long as possible, i.e., 60 - 90 days after the contract has been signed. This extended period will allow you plenty of time to close your loan on your old home and to make the necessary arrangements for moving, etc. During this time period, while you are waiting for your present home to close and fund, you have successfully stopped the price of your new home from increasing another 1% per month. Sometimes it makes economic sense to pay the seller's current asking price if the seller will agree to delay closing for up to 90 days.

CHAPTER THREE

Have a Clear Goal for Selling Your Home

"A house divided against itself cannot stand."
-- Abraham Lincoln

One of the most costly mistakes we continue to see in any market--whether the market is booming or declining—is the way sellers handle the entire affair without ever considering what the process will be and what the goal is for the family. Which is why I've seen pride, stubbornness and tempers kill more deals than any one factor simply because the seller did not take the time to think about the purpose and goal of selling the home. Be aware that failing to establish clear goals before you market your home could result in not being able to sell or even in **foreclosure**.

If it weren't so sad, it would almost be funny to see just how emotional sellers often become over issues that have nothing to do with their primary goal. It is no secret that pricing the home properly influences the quality and quantity of potential buyers who will be inspecting your home over the next few months. Being focused and ready to deal with any offer can turn selling your home into a very positive experience.

Even during a declining market, buyers are transferred—they move, die, divorce, scale up or down, which means that real estate continues to trade owners, regardless of market conditions.

The key issue our firm had to deal with during the Texas real estate tumble was not producing buyers and offers, but rather that sellers still were not properly prepared to sell their home. **Remember the only market you have is the one you are in at the present time.**

How To Get Your Act Together and Save Money in the Process

Here is a simple goal-setting process that we suggest you follow prior to putting your home on the market. While it may seem easy at first glance, you must be able to produce a clearly-defined, written purpose for selling and what commitments you will make to insure that success.

1) **What is the goal of selling?** Don't confuse this question with why you want to sell.
   Is the goal to:
   a) recover your equity?
   b) move to another community?
   c) upsize/downsize?
   d) make a profit?
   e) avoid foreclosure?
   f) liquidate for divorce?
   g) estate-forced sale?
   k) Other: _____

2) **What is the current real estate market condition?**

   Do your homework first! Use actual knowledge only, no rumors or unqualified sources. Watch for newspaper stories with actual graphs of sales, number of listings, closings and average sales price. Is it declining, steady, improving? The current market is:_____

   _____

   _____

   _____

3) **Why do you want to sell? Who or what is the motivating factor? Is the entire family in agreement with the sale? Are economics a factor?**

   We want to sell because: _____

   _____

   _____

   _____

   _____

4) **What is our commitment level to making our home sell?**

   In list form, make a clear statement of your willingness to paint, fix up, organize, repair.

   _____

   _____

   _____

5) **If your agent has a video tape to show you how to make ready your home, will you watch, listen and act?**
(This is a simple yes/no by all parties.)
Yes _____   No _____

6) **Are you willing to listen to expert advice about the listing price and expenses you will incur to sell your home?**
Yes _____   No _____

7) **What is the financial goal that you want to realize from the sale of your home?**
Actual amount: _____

How did you arrive at this amount?

_____

_____

8) **If you fail to reach your projected financial goal, are you willing to set a new goal?**
Yes _____   No _____

9) **If you fail to sell your home in the next 30, 60, 90 days, what will happen to your equity in terms of dollars?**

_____

_____

_____

10) What process will you use to select your agent?
(See Chapter Six before you answer this question.)

_____

_____

_____

_____

CHAPTER FOUR

Don't List Your Home with the Real Estate Agent/Broker Who Quotes the Highest Price!

It's one of the oldest tricks in the book: Real Estate Agent/Broker quotes the owner the highest price during the listing interview because the owner has already placed a higher perceived value (Mistake #1) on his or her home than what it is actually worth.

Since most owners overprice their home prior to meeting the Real Estate Agent/Broker, here is how they set themselves up for wanting the highest possible price.

First, they may talk to neighbors who sold their home last month. Most homeowners I've worked with are generally honest people, but to tell the truth, when it comes to disclosing to neighbors how much they got for their home, it's amazing how exaggerated the selling price becomes. In fact, most sellers just can't bear letting their neighbor know exactly what the home sold for. Their conversation may sound something like this once their home is listed and goes under contract:

Neighbor #1: "I see you sold your home."

Neighbor #2: "I never thought we'd be able to sell it for the price we did."

Neighbor #1: "Oh, so you were happy about the selling price?"

Neighbor #2: "You bet! We got everything we expected and then some."

Neighbor #1: "You're kidding! That's great. How much did you sell it for?"

Neighbor #2: "More than we ever imagined! Can't wait for it to close next month."

Now Neighbor #1's mind is reeling from the conversation because he or she knows that if Neighbor #2 sold their home for the listing price then his or her home is worth that much more.

Second, they imagine their home is worth more money because it has better amenities. Owners immediately jump into the Mistake #1 mode again by allowing emotion and pride to cloud their judgment. We have never had or known a seller who didn't believe in their hearts that their home was better or bigger than a neighbor's who sold down the street. (Sound familiar?)

Your particular home's amenities, such as a larger game room or basement, may be the selling point or reason you purchased it in the first place, but the buyers who are considering your home may place a higher priority on an extra large master bedroom and a more modern bathroom. The game room may not be necessary for a prospective buyer, so he or she will see less value in your home if the master suite is too small. Remember, buyers only purchase homes that fit their needs.

Third, most sellers talk to their friends or co-workers seeking free advice prior to listing their homes. Most of the time these conversations are filled with additional rumors about other homes that sold for higher prices. This leads the seller to make statements to the Real Estate Agent/Broker which paint themselves into a corner without realizing it, such as "I am not going to list my house under $150,000" which will make it impossible for the Agent/Broker to do their job when the listing appointment is made. Real Estate agents—like most people—do not handle rejection well. Often, they'll accept an over-priced listing just to please the seller, even when they know in their heart that the home will never sell for that price.

After the data gathering has been done, the seller is now ready to interview several Real Estate Agent/Brokers to determine the listing price.

Hiring the Wrong Agent

Real Estate Agent/Broker #1: Makes an outstanding listing presentation, including an excellent marketing program, and quotes a price lower than the sellers perceived price, but one which reflects time on the market and current market conditions.

Real Estate Agent/Broker #2: Makes the listing presentation which shows the history of the market and quotes a price 10% above or below current market to allow time for the property to sell. Depending on market conditions, the Realtor may add 10% for an improving market or subtract 10% for a declining market.

Real Estate Agent/Broker #3: Quotes the current market but gives the seller credit for repairs and amenities which results in a slightly higher price than the seller was expecting.

Thus, Real Estate Agent/Broker #3 gets the listing. The reason is twofold:

a) The listing price meets or beats the other two Real Estate Agent/Broker's price,

b) It allows the seller to be a hero at home and in the office because the home is listed at the price that he or she perceives the value to be.

It is very hard for the seller to resist listing the home with the Real Estate Agent who quotes the highest price and extra credits for amenities. It is critical to avoid this overpricing trap if the seller wants to prevent the possibility of not selling the home at all. **The goal is to sell the home.** The correct price is absolutely crucial to finding a buyer quickly.

The quickest way to make Mistake #2 "Overpricing Your Home" is to deny what current market conditions are doing. Nothing is wrong with being optimistic about the market, but to hold out for that one buyer who will meet your price could result in never selling your home or losing your home to **foreclosure.** This is especially true if selling your home is a critical issue because for whatever reason you have to move, i.e., job transfers won't wait several years for your home to sell. It's certainly not worth putting your family under stress for the extra dollars, and above all, remember that asking the higher price can easily result in the home staying on the market for a long time and maybe in never being sold.

It is a common practice for some Real Estate Agents to take overpriced listings knowing the property will never sell at that price. They know that in 90-120 days you will come around and lower your price. This practice enables the agent to control the listing and patiently wait for you to become discouraged enough to approve the new sales price that you should have started with at the beginning of the listing period.

Homes quickly develop a stigma or reputation if they are on the market for a long period of time. One of the first questions a buyer will ask the Agent/Broker is, "How long has this home been listed?". If the property has been on the market for 90-120 days, the very next question the buyer will most likely will ask is, "What's wrong with it?". It is not uncommon for property that has been on the market for an extended period to be discussed by other Real Estate Agents/Brokers in other companies. These agents can usually pinpoint the problem quickly. Invariably the problem is that (a) the property is over-priced for the market or (b) the property does not show well. It is cluttered, dirty, outdated or difficult to show, i.e. dogs, cats or the owner is always present. Sometimes the owner or tenant is uncooperative.

Having to overcome any of these circumstances will make it almost impossible for the Agent/Broker to reach the homeowner's goal of selling the home. Always remember that price will motivate the majority of buyers. Even the worst fixer-upper can attract many offers if the price is right.

So if your house has been sitting on the market for 90-120 days without an acceptable offer, something is wrong. It's time to discuss a new marketing plan with your Agent/Broker. I strongly recommend that you have that person call as many of the Real Estate Agents/ Brokers as possible who have previewed or shown your home to a buyer. You need to obtain feedback from them. It is critical that you ask your listing Agent/Broker for candid comments. You will not like or appreciate some of what is said, but you must, nevertheless, consider it carefully. Listen with an objective, open mind rather than reacting with emotion. This process may be difficult for you, however, it will hold the key to why your home has not sold.

If you are receiving only positive feedback, then again , something is not right. Either the Agent/Broker is afraid of your reaction or is not asking the right questions of the other Agents/Brokers. Press your Agent/Broker for any negative comments, then go about correcting the problems and concerns quickly. **Remember that negative comments come from potential buyers.**

If a price change is in order, I recommend that you take your home off the market for two or three days, then enter a new listing at the new price. Many multiple listing services re-assign a new listing number which indicates how long the property has been listed by the sequence of numbers. Property that has been on the market for a long period of time has a lower listing number. Your new number and listing price will reflect renewed enthusiasm and energy to get it sold this time around.

CHAPTER FIVE

Chasing the Market Downhill and Testing a Slow or Improving Market

This may be the hardest mistake to avoid simply because most owners refuse to believe that the market has: (a) declined as much as the facts indicate and, (b) that the market will continue to decline.

Here in Austin, Texas, our residential market peaked in 1985 and then continued to decline for the next five years. In some parts of the city home values declined as much as 40-50% depending on location and condition of the house. Our associates talked to hundreds of homeowners who wanted to sell during those years only to see their perceived equity diminish. Many of these homes went into foreclosure simply because owners could not lease the property without having to bring hundreds of dollars to the table each month to meet the mortgage payment. Most of these homeowners started out optimistically—they thought they would be able to sell, until they saw the market continue its downward slide.

Their initial optimism is fueled by the belief that their home is worth more, is different (or special) from other homes in the neighborhood (see Chapters 2 and 3) and that a prospective buyer will be eager to pay the old market value before the prices decline.

Chasing the market downhill actually is very easy to do because most owners are determined to establish a listing price slightly over the current market conditions so they will be able to negotiate with the buyer when an offer does present itself.

Buyers become extremely knowledgeable in a declining market and you must understand the reason why. Let's say you are a buyer for a home listed in your price range and neighborhood. What would be your first step toward finding the right home for you and your family at the very best price? You would invariably look at what's on the market and what is the best deal. If two homes were equal in size, amenities and condition, but one was priced $5,000 more than the other home, which owner would you begin your negotiations with? A vast majority of buyers will choose the home with the lowest price for several reasons.

1) The house is priced closest to current market conditions. It represents a better value.

2) The price tells the buyer that the owner with the lower listed price understands the current market conditions, and it will probably be easier to arrive at a price that suits both buyer and seller.

3) Most buyers really don't want to hassle
    with a determined seller, and they will
    usually go the route of least resistance.
    That is why they ask questions such as,
    how long has the home been on the
    market and how motivated is the seller?
    or, why is the owner moving?

Buyers fully understand that they are in the best possible position during a declining market. While home prices are falling, rents and leases in the area usually follow the same trend, especially if an area has been hard hit by a business recession, i.e., large employer layoffs or plant closings.

Economic conditions convey an underlying message in most communities, and many buyers are understandably reluctant to purchase a home until the recession is over.

It is during this particular down market period that the buyer can take all the time he or she desires because waiting will only benefit the buyer. A declining market is a buyer's paradise.

Motivated sellers also have some options, and that is why it is critical for the seller to outline a game plan for attracting buyers. In Chapter 7 and 10 we will discuss marketing and presentation of the home, but right now let's discuss the number one reason why owners lose buyers before they even have a chance to negotiate a contract.

Price, Price, Price!

Some owners may not be able to reduce their listing price to current market conditions simply because the declining market has eroded their equity. If that's the case, you may seriously want to consider keeping your home or turning it into a rental property.

When you list your home below the market value, it attracts buyers even if your home doesn't fit their needs. Remember that buyers talk to family, friends, co-workers, et al. when they earnestly begin looking for a home. Although they may not be interested in your home, they could pass on to another buyer information about your home.

Price is the one controlling factor in a slow market! In a slow/depreciating market nothing beats a bargain price. NOTHING!

Don't Test a Slow, Static or Improving Market

The best advice I can give you is that setting your price to "test the market" or to leave yourself "negotiating room" will cost you in the actual number of buyers who look at your home and will certainly determine if you receive any offers to purchase.

The best rule I can give you is to set your lowest price and stick with it. I've seen more contracts accepted at full asking price than you can imagine because the owner was willing to list under the current market prices. Buyers can recognize a bargain, and they love to talk about the "great deal" they found. Nothing excites a buyer more than an opportunity to purchase a home priced under the current market. Pricing works in all markets!

Listing your home at a reasonable price will prove to be your most important decision in the entire selling process.

It really doesn't matter if your market is in a boom or bust cycle, the buyer must believe that your home represents a bargain in the market at that time.

The mistake I see and hear about in a boom market is the seller's belief that they sold too cheap or should have squeezed out another $500/$1,000 from the buyers.

The most common error made by a seller is thinking the buyer won't walk a contract once they have started negotiating for a property. Wrong! Pushing a buyer for more money in an improving market usually is the one thing that makes a contract fall off or fail because buyers are scared to pay too much for a property. The least hint of hitting a fixed ceiling on what they are willing to pay may stop the negotiations totally. It's easy for the buyer to wait or halt contract negotiations over $250. We all have a fear of paying too much!

Buyers are always nervous about price, especially if they are concerned with the probability of the market slowing down in the future. No one wants to pay top dollar for a home only to see the market take a down turn in the next few years.

My advice to any homeowner is to make the best deal possible without losing the buyer in the process.

Holding out for the last dollar doesn't matter if you lose the buyer.

Remember, in any market the buyer determines the price.

CHAPTER SIX

Choosing the Wrong and Right Real Estate Agent/Broker

Once you understand how real estate companies normally operate you will have a better insight when picking the Real Estate Agent/Broker/Firm who can help you the most.

The quickest way to make a mistake in finding the right Real Estate Agent/Broker is to start with the assumption that the top listing Real Estate Agent/Broker in town is the person you want to handle your sale.

The second fastest way to make a mistake is to go after the largest firm or biggest national franchise Real Estate Agent/Broker in your area.

REMEMBER THIS RULE: If either the company or the agent is advertising that they are Number One - look for "you" in that ad. You need a company that considers you first. You're Number One. SERVICE TO YOU IS THE KEY.

Many real estate professionals who produce record sales in excess of $8 to 10 million shoulder a huge burden of responsibility. Under normal conditions, a sales associate can handle about 20 to 25 transactions per year without having an assistant to act as a backup while they are out of the office, on appointments, etc.

Very few of those top producers limit their goals because most are driven/motivated to strive for excellence, recognition and money. If they sold $8 to 10 million worth of property last year, then a higher goal is sought this year. Many will increase their personal goals and hire additional assistants until they max out or destroy their health or personal life or both. The tenure of a real estate associate is not long according to the National Association of Realtors. The average tenure is less than ten years.

Top producers want to please their customers, but most are just too busy to pay attention to a seller who might need special attention. If a top producer fails to sell your home, it's just one more listing not sold that year. But to you it can mean a devastating blow to your financial and emotional well-being.

Let's say that a top producer who has sales of $8 to 10 million per year, will handle between 80 to 100 closed transactions per year (if the average sales of homes is $100,000-$125,000). This particular Real Estate Agent/ Broker may be working with over 12 transactions per month, and that could be as high as 19 different couples or families on a monthly basis due to overlapping appointments and closings. On an average this Real Estate Agent/ Broker will handle in two months what it takes an above-average Real Estate Agent/Broker to handle in 12 months.

Have you ever been rushed while purchasing merchandise? Remember that feeling you had towards the clerk? Did you feel rushed or unappreciated? that you, the customer, did not come first? Just imagine what it will be like when the biggest financial decision you will probably ever make is rushed through so that the salesperson can go on to the next contact.

If you must sell your home, I would recommend that you skip the top producers simply because they may not have the extra time to spend planning a proper marketing approach for your home. Top producers are trained to sell quickly. If they miss on one deal, they are more prone to say "next." **You will be treated no differently.**

The best overall sales people I have seen are the above-average producers who normally sell $3 to 4 million per year. They seem the best organized and less stressed of all of the Real Estate Agent/Brokers. For them, it is family first, job second. They also have a reputation for handling their business in a more personal manner. They tend to give their clients more attention and respect, i.e., service.

When you interview a Real Estate Agent/Broker, you should look for a pattern of success. Find out how long they've been in the business or if they are new to real estate. What is their background, what are their successes in their prior business? I would even accept an experienced business person who happens to be new to real estate, if that person had a history of achievement in their past employment and a plan to get your home sold. Be sure to send for our checklist of 10 major questions to ask when interviewing your potential Real Estate Agent/Broker. See back page for order form.

CHAPTER SEVEN

Before You Sign a Listing Agreement

The Number One goal of a real estate agent is to procure an "Exclusive Right to Sell" Listing Agreement with you. **Therefore, never sign a listing agreement without first negotiating the stated promises.** You must agree upon everything up front.

Most good agents today will make a presentation that includes information about the company, sales records, number of listings and more flattering details about the agent than you ever need to know or want to hear.

How to Discover the Agent's Goal

Usually sellers start the home selling process long before an agent is contacted. Typically, most people will ask business associates, family and friends to recommend someone who they've had good luck with—someone they can trust.

Other sellers will watch neighborhood real estate signs to see who is listing many of the homes. Still others rely upon the reputation of the major national franchise companies. Then, of course, there's always the yellow pages for selecting a company.

All of These Methods Could Prove to be a Disaster!

Discovering the goal of the agent is really quite easy. Most agents have a "canned" presentation of "yes" questions and procedures to go through to get you to list now! In fact agents attend all types of seminars that train them to develop a drill style for their listing presentation.

Trust Your Instincts First

When selecting an agent, he or she should be someone you feel good about, someone whom you're willing to trust with the biggest financial transaction you may ever engage in. And since it involves your family, you want to be secure in the knowledge that the agent has your best interest at heart. Here are just a few things to check out before you arrive at the place where you're ready to sign on the dotted line and begin the process of selling your home. Any agent who shows concern for the delay that your further checking might create is automatically suspect.

It's Homework Time!

Before signing any listing agreement:

1) Ask for references from past sellers. Flattering letters praising the agent's work—letters provided in a presentation book—are a great start, but **dig deeper**. Ask for the telephone

numbers and names of the past three sellers and at least two current listings.

2) Ask your family, friends and business associates about the company or agent and listen carefully for the very first thing they will say. A company has a reputation in the community. Listen for it.

3) Call the Real Estate Commission and ask about any consumer complaints. **Note of caution**: Most major real estate companies will have more customer complaints during a slow or declining market simply because that is human nature. No real estate company ever gets sued or has complaints filed against it when the seller or buyer reaps a large profit from the sale. That's because the customer's ego comes into play. If the transaction is financially beneficial, the customer's attitude is "See how smart I was." But let the market dip in value and suddenly the customer is looking for an anchor to hang onto or someone to blame for the misfortune. Because a company or agent has complaints does not necessarily mean they are unethical or that they are not a company to do business with. The more transactions they handle the larger the exposure to having suits or complaints.

4) Call the Better Business Bureau to see if this company has any records of bad dealings with their customers.

5) Ask for the agent's and the company's record on innovations in the marketplace. How are they dealing with the current housing market? Is there a plan to beef up their advertising or structure the marketing program that most benefits the seller? A company in a temporary transition may still be the company to list with. A temporary transition means that the company is in the middle of reorganizing their sales staff or marketing program. Residential Real Estate has a long history of economic cycles. The market is either hot, improving, static or declining, and with each cycle there has to be a plan to cope with the current market.

Ask, Ask, Ask

Ask to see charts of sales compared to one year ago. How is the agent and company doing? **Ask for a real estate tenure history of the agent.** Does this agent jump ship all the time? How many different companies has he/she worked for? What were the reasons he/she left? (Note: if the reason is always money, check your gut instinct-- **something is wrong!**) Any agent who continues to change brokerage companies will leave this one if a better offer comes along. Your listing belongs to the broker. That means you will either be assigned a new agent or the broker will maintain the listing. Be aware that this could disrupt the marketing program if the agent is planning to leave.

One Further Caution: If the agent tells you confidentially of plans to leave and tries to encourage you to delay your listing, **LOOK AGAIN** at this agent, particularly if loyalty is an important issue with you. If the agent can't be loyal when working for a broker, how loyal will he or she be with your listing?

In a recent radio talk show interview, a new Real Estate Agent was quite upset that I was recommending that home sellers look at the Agent's/Broker's tenure in the business when selecting a professional to list their home. He went on to say that many Agents/Brokers who have been in the business for some time have become lazy and sloppy. In fact, he said they won't hold open houses as quickly as new Agents and certainly are not as enthusiastic as someone who is new to the business. My response to his criticism was that I agree with his points, however, the selection process by the seller should include the tenure issue only as part of the Agent's/Broker's overall qualifications. Some of the best Real Estate Agents I know have been in the business less than eighteen months. To help balance the experience or inexperience issue for the seller, you must understand that the selection of the listing Agent/Broker is critical to your success. This person is your representative by law. He or she has a fiduciary responsibility to protect your interests above all others. If the new Agent/Broker has a reliable company to help forge the way and you trust this individual, then go with that person, but require some standards of performace during the first 30-60 days of representation.

Final Questions to Ask Before You Sign

1) **Ask for a detailed marketing plan** with a step-by-step outline of what the agent will do during the first four weeks that your home is on the market eight weeks, twelve weeks. (See our order form "10 Tips To a Successful Marketing Plan" in the back of this book.)

2) **Ask for an escape clause** allowing you to cancel the agreement if the agent or company does not live up to the marketing plan. Waiting until your listing agreement is up will only cost you money in a declining market.

3) **Limit the listing term** to 60 days with an automatic renewal for 60 additional days. Most agents will tell you it's company policy to list for six months. Tell them no and explain that the reason is because you are a serious seller—one who is willing to

put in writing what you intend to do to assist the agent in procuring a contract. **Remember, this effort is a joint venture to find a qualified buyer.**

4) **Define planning times.** Establish a calendar with your agent to go over the marketing results within the first 15 days. Ask for all showings, feedback from other agents, etc. Help the agent to understand that any news is good even if it's bad because it helps you to make adjustments in your marketing plan or create a whole new one.

If objections to your price continue to come up in the planning discussions, then you must anticipate the future. Drop the price immediately and make sure the new price will be below market conditions for 60 days. Pricing is critical to your success!

8 Tips On How to Help Your Agent Produce Results

Seller's agreement: You, too, must be willing to commit your resources to get your home sold. Along with all of the other items in Chapter Seven, you should absolutely do the following:

1) Listen to your agent.

2) Make the house "Model House" ready.

3) Fix the items that are broken.

4) Remove all pets (Yes, I love pets, but not everyone does).

5) Remove your entire family when a buyer is present.

6) Don't negotiate with a buyer no matter how great the temptation, unless it's written in your contract with the agent.

7) Be flexible on all offers.

8) List the property below current market value, if possible.

Tell your agent if he or she signs the marketing plan, you will sign the above agreement in order to encourage offers on your property.

CHAPTER EIGHT

It Pays to Advertise

Don't let the Real Estate Agent/Broker talk you out of an advertising program for your home! Advertising does work!

When you call in an expert to sell your home you should expect professional advice, yet every year thousands of sellers are shown pie charts and surveys to convince them that buyers don't come from advertising in the newspaper. Wrong!

Real Estate Agent/Brokers attend seminars and company training programs which systematically insist that advertising doesn't work. In fact, most of an agent's ad budget is centered around promotions extolling the benefits of working with that agent and how many multi-million dollars' worth of real estate he or she has sold.

The reason why real estate advertising programs and their ads don't work is because not nearly enough time is spent on developing an effective advertising campaign. Plus, when you start out training a sales staff to believe that newspaper ads are not cost effective, the end result is pretty obvious. Newspaper advertising doesn't work and can't work in a negative environment.

Buyers read newspaper ads regularly, and they will respond to a properly written ad.

Before you sign an agreement to list your home, have a clear understanding of exactly what type of advertising program you want. (See marketing list on next page.)

Our marketing department at Easter & Easter is small but we enjoy an outstanding reputation for producing an unprecedented amount of responses. One ad (2" width x 4") recently brought us 75 prospective customers.

It is not uncommon for our firm to register 25 calls directly from an ad, particularly if the copy is good and catches the buyer's eye.

This classified heading, along with additional copy, produced over six showings in one day and resulted in a contract for the seller.

Grandma's House

Step into yesteryear where Grandma's memories abound. Beautiful hardwood floors, wonderful custom craftsmanship woodwork throughout. Front door screens and covered porches will make you stay forever. Call Now!

This classified ad produced over 100 calls in a four-week time period.

Basketball Court Size Bedrooms

You won't believe how large these King Kong size bedrooms are! Perfect for a giant's family or someone who has TONS of furniture/clothes. Walkie-talkies included in sales price. Bring checkbook before this big bargain is gone. (P.S. The bedrooms are not basketball court size, but they are huge!)

Ask The Agent:
1) Who writes the ads for your company?
2) What is their background?

If they fail to address this critical issue, **ask again** and don't proceed until you have an answer. You are looking for innovation and expertise.

How To Find an Innovative Marketing Professional

The easiest and best way to locate a real estate company that is not afraid to attract buyers via newspaper advertising is to take your Sunday newspaper and circle every headline that actually makes you read the ad. If you use different colored pens for each company involved, it will soon become apparent how innovative the more aggressive firms are. Pick one that motivates you with their ad copy.

Advertising alone cannot carry the burden of selling your home. The buyer's attention must be grabbed and held by the uniqueness of the ad copy. That's why it's critical to check out the style of advertising before you sign the listing agreement.

A good marketing plan will include a fast start of advertising to lure the most potential buyers. In fact, research studies show that the first two to three weeks are critical periods for a home to receive its best and most qualified prospective customers.

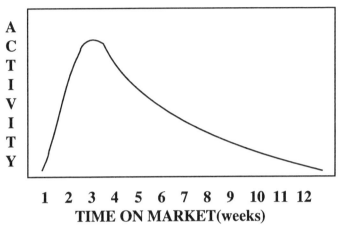

Source: Better Homes & Gardens, The Home Marketing System - © 1990, Meredith Corporation.

Always remember the Golden Rule. Those who have the Gold make the rules, and in a real estate market, the buyers have the Gold!

The second biggest mistake—after over pricing—is not having an effective marketing plan to launch your campaign to sell your home.

Other Ways to Advertise

Newspaper should not be your only advertising strategy. The fact is that most good Real Estate Agent/Brokers use a wide variety of marketing tools to deliver the message of excellent homes for sale.

Direct mail is a critical method of advertising, along with special publications printed exclusively for Real Estate buyers. Your local area Brokers may advertise their homes on a weekly or bi-weekly calendar using color photograph ads or black and white copy. Most of these magazines are circulated free to grocery stores and other locations.

Remember the real estate company has but one goal when they advertise a home: **to make the phone ring.**

Homes selected to be advertised are studied to see which ad will produce the most results. Many homeowners fail to understand that their home will most likely not be advertised often, or at all, if the price and location is not a sufficient drawing card. (Remember Chapter 2.)

Does that mean that a company has failed the owner if the home is not being advertised every week? Absolutely not!

Why A Home Is Not Advertised

If your home is not being advertised, this is an indication of several scenarios: (1) the company or agent believes that your price is too high, (2) the office uses a rotation basis for advertising listings and your turn is not up yet or (3) the company is having budget constraints. While this may be true in some cases, the homes that usually cause the phone to ring are the ones that have the best price.

A Real Estate Broker normally will pick the best home to advertise in order to bring in prospective-buyer calls for the company. These calls should be screened to determine the buyers' needs and income levels. Most Real Estate Agents show every home on the market in a potential buyer's price range. A majority of incoming buyers' calls never see the home they have called about simply because it was not in the neighborhood or not the style of home they were interested in purchasing.

How do you know if your Real Estate Agent/ Broker's advertising/marketing plan is working? Count the number of cards and showings from other Real Estate Agenst/Brokers. You should have a good mixture of other real estate firms previewing and showing your home. If not, ask your Real Estate Agent/Broker for a checklist of items where the home is being exposed. If, in fact, your home is being marketed correctly, you must immediately take action to adjust your price until you start receiving acceptable offers that reflect current market conditions.

Check For These Activities And Follow Ups:

1) Direct mail feature sheets to successful agents.
2) Direct mail to other listing agents who have listings in subject home's area.
3) Number of ads in newspapers, other print media.
4) Comments from other Real Estate Agents about your home.
5) Comments from buyers who have seen your property.

It is not uncommon for your Agent/Broker to avoid steps 4 and 5 because the feedback about your home could cause some conflict. To get a clear picture of how well your home is being accepted by the real estate community and potential buyers, it is necesary for you to be objective and non-judgemental about comments from these two sources. If a home is receiving negative comments from both of these sources, no amount of advertising will overcome the issues. Asking your Agent/Broker to continue to advertise a home that is drawing unfavorable comments will only result in wasting both of your time and efforts.

Find out what the issues are and correct the problems. When the home is ready to be advertised again, be sure the new improvements are clearly reflected in the ad copy. **Price reduction should not be part of the new advertising copy** because it indicates to the buyer that the home has been on the market for some time. I recommend the new advertising copy include the amenities and benefits of the property. The price should speak for itself, and the buyer will know if it is a fair price.

CHAPTER NINE

Taking Your Home Off the Market Too Soon

I suggest you mark this chapter and re-read it whenever an offer is presented for your consideration because if you take your home off the market before you find out if the buyer is qualified, you are **negotiating to lose.**

Many states do not allow Real Estate Agent/ Brokers to negotiate with the seller or write the offer for the buyer. **Therefore, this chapter is not legal advice and should not be construed as such.** If you have any questions about information in this chapter, you should consult your attorney or legal representative for real estate.

First of all, an offer by a buyer is an inquiry to the seller to see if the two parties can come to terms over the differences of opinion about the worth of the seller's property and other conditions, such as, financing, closing, possession, etc. This stage is critical because many sellers wind up venting their anger on the prospective buyer because many of them start their negotiations with a much lower offer than the selling price and often include too many other requests or requirements which will cost the seller more money than was anticipated when the home went on the market.

In some states, Real Estate Agents/Brokers are required by law to present all offers to the seller up to the date of closing. This means that **any** offer has to be presented even **after** the buyer and seller have agreed on terms and the contracts have been executed. This particular requirement to present contracts to a seller after the seller has accepted an offer on his/her property has been interpreted differently across the United States. In 1992, the Texas Real Estate Commission stated that presenting an offer after an agreement has been reached is the Broker's option. The National Association of Realtors encouraged Brokers to address the issue with sellers in the listing agreement. The Real Estate Agent/Broker still has to present extremely low offers. **Don't react to a low starting point offer!** Stepping into the buyers shoes will help you understand why the buyer has asked for so many considerations: **Buyers take the attitude that if you don't ask, you don't receive.**

So instead of balking at the reduced offer, systematically take it apart by putting an actual dollar value on each item. If the buyer has asked for things which were excluded in the listing agreement, stop and put a value on that particular item and then ask yourself: What can I trade this for in the contract? Usually if something has been singled out by the buyer, it is an important issue. For instance, maybe the dining room chandelier was not included, but the buyer now demands that it stay with the home. Most sellers fail to realize that the chandelier could have been the **reason** why the buyer started considering the home in the first place. If the formal dining room projects a certain look and feel, it may have spurred dreams of future parties or family gatherings under the lights of the chandelier. And that special feeling which the buyer had might disappear if the homeowners attempt to take the fixture with them. **(If you do not want an item to convey a certain look or emotional quality, replace it before you start showing your home.)**

The purchase of residential real estate property is usually based on an emotion. Potential buyers become anxious to purchase when the home delivers or meets their expectations of future happiness and dreams. Taking those feelings away or diminishing them by negotiating about a light fixture could be very unwise. Instead, leave the fixture in place and negotiate a cash payment for it just as you would for repair considerations or a title policy.

Remember, when a buyer takes the time and effort to write an offer on your home, there is considerable interest. Find out from your Real Estate Agent/Broker what the buyer really likes, and use that as an area which will encourage negotiations to continue rather than come to a standstill.

Before negotiations reach the agreement stage, there is one extremely important rule to follow: **Never take your home off the market before you find out if the buyer is qualified.**

Warning: A letter from any lender or mortgage company is not a commitment to loan money. It is only an opinion stating that if the facts presented by the buyers are true, the loan may be approved and processed. This letter is not an agreement to make a loan.

All too often in a slow market, sellers are so eager to get their home sold that any offer is welcomed with a sigh of relief, even if it is not the full asking price and the terms are not quite what the owners had in mind.

Each buyer will have a price range of homes they can afford. Many times Real Estate Agents/Brokers do not —or will not—ask the following imperative questions:

1) How long have the buyers been employed at their current jobs?
2) What is their income?
3) Is part of their income based on commission sales or bonuses? If so, what is their net income if self-employed?
4) How much long-term debt are the buyers carrying?
5) Have the buyers been pre-qualified for a loan?
6) Is the credit report clean? Are there any problems?

If the buyers have been pre-qualified, request a written verification from the manager of the mortgage company, bank or lender.

Some sellers think that asking such questions about the financial condition of the buyers invades their privacy. There are certain laws which protect consumers, and it is important to keep from violating those laws. But the reason to ask for financial information is to insure that the sale will close once both parties agree on terms and conditions.

I've seen so many sales transactions lost because the real estate agent and owner were afraid to ask these necessary, qualifying questions. They may seem tough at first, but you or your agent must ask them and receive satisfactory answers. Don't sign any agreement until you are confident that the buyers are qualified to purchase your home. Once an agreement has been signed it might take months and cause you to incur legal expenses to get out of a contract if the buyer is not qualified.

Failure to address these issues up front can:
1) cost you thousands of dollars,
2) delay the sale of your home and,
3) put you on an emotional roller coaster.

If your home is off the market for 60 to 90 days—especially during the peak season—and you have to put it back on the market because the buyer didn't qualify, think about the loss of time, the drop in value in a declining market, plus the anxiety of not knowing whether you should pack or stay. Learn to ask the tough questions before signing a contract.

If You Have an Assumable Loan -Watch Out!
Warning: If your present loan is assumable, you must understand that by allowing a buyer to purchase your home without going through a formal approval process with the current mortgage company, may mean that the

new buyer's failure to make the payments could come back to haunt you in the future. Ask your **attorney** to inform you of the legal issues involved when someone assumes your loan without the qualifying procedure.

Here's the way it works: In a declining market, buyers may see their down payment equity vanish in a year, and if the market continues to slide, there is little incentive for the new owners to keep making payments especially if rental rates are following the same market trends and they can house their family for $100 to 200 less than the current mortgage payment on their new home.

Equity plays an important role in determining which homes are given back to the lender. **The larger the equity the more effort is made to keep the property.**

During the real estate recession in Texas, there were serious scams going on in which fraudulent buyers would purchase homes with assumable loans that did not require qualifying. Then they would rent the homes to tenants, collect the rent and never make a payment. In most contracts, the buyer would ask the seller for the refrigerator, washer and dryer (in some states these appliances automatically come with the mortgage) and they would ask the seller to make the next two mortgage payments to insure the necessary time for the new buyer to lease the property. Thus, the buyer immediately leases the property, under market, collects the rent and never makes a payment. Since the mortgage company usually took six months or more before they foreclosed on the property, this added up to a nice profit for the new buyers. Several persons in Texas were sentenced to prison for fraud for these scams; however, it took years to catch the scam artists, and in the process, many suffered without hopes of recovery.

So: Let the seller beware. If you allow someone to assume your loan, make sure you check references and their credit. Check past history of homes owned and past rental history. Spend the necessary time and money to have your attorney advise you during this process. In the long run, it will save you time and money-- and grief.

CHAPTER TEN

Nailing Down the Big Issues

Failing to ask for enough escrow and setting time limits for financing are vitally important issues. Homeowners seldom realize the necessity of demanding enough escrow to maintain the contract between the time of signing and closing the transaction. Once again, the seller is more concerned with the price of the property than the end result of closing the deal 30, 60 or 90 days down the road.

When a market is declining in value, it is not uncommon to see buyers trying to obtain property with as little cash as possible. **Never, absolutely never, take your home off the market without adequate escrow fees.** Two percent of the sales price is the very minimum amount you should ask for. Five percent is middle range. Ten percent would be ideal, but that amount could raise a warning sign to the buyers, especially if they have concerns about repairs, the neighborhood or financing.

How and Why You Should Ask
For a Large Escrow Deposit

Remember, buyers today are very knowledgeable about purchasing a home. Most have some working knowledge of the process, and a great majority absolutely know the current market and prices better than most sellers. While sellers seem to think they are more current about the market than buyers, remember that the buyers may have been in and out of homes for the past two or three months. Buyers are in the driver's seat. In a declining market, they are apt to wait--as decreasing prices are to their benefit. In a boom market, they'll want to lock in a fixed sales price--again to their benefit.

If a buyer can negotiate a home for the price they want to pay, and with the terms, conditions and financing they want, they will attempt to make one last effort to win the best position possible by submitting a small escrow fund. Here is the reason why:

The smaller the escrow, the quicker the buyer will default if the market continues to decline or if another home catches their eye.

Many buyers continue to shop for other homes even when they are under contract for another home. **Surprise, Surprise!**

It was not uncommon during our declining market to see buyers who were under contract and in the process of obtaining a loan for one property, attending open houses and calling on ads in the newspapers. Buyers have the know-how and knowledge to get around most skilled agents. Occasionally, our most seasoned associates would be caught off guard when a prospective buyer would finally confess they were "just shopping" to see if they missed any real bargains or if they could find a better deal. These conversations would eventually come up when our associates actually did find a better deal for the buyers and the buyers would start asking questions about getting out of their other contract. When we first started encountering these situations it really caught us by surprise. In Texas, since it is against the law for real estate agents to practice law or give legal advice, we responded to these buyers by saying, "You need to seek legal counsel."

Our professional ethics also demanded that we suggest that the buyer should shop with our competition since we now had knowledge that would be harmful to any seller who might consider a contract with these buyers. If a buyer will back out once, they will back out twice. We didn't want to be a party to any such deal.

A Small Escrow Fund Puts You in a Bad Position

A small escrow allows the buyer to continue to shop while they have your home off of the market and under legal contract. If the buyer finds a better price, location, or bigger house during the process, they are in a much better position to walk out of your contract. Here is why:

1) Their loan application is progressing the whole time they're under contract. The closer the loan application is to being approved, the stronger their position becomes if they find another property. Once a buyer is approved for a loan, he/she can switch the loan to another property. The lender is approving the loan amount, not the purchase

of a specific house. It is true, however, that a new appraisal must be ordered for the new property.

2) They can actually be shopping while your house is off the market.

3) Should they find a better deal, they could negotiate another purchase with an escape clause such as, "This contract is contingent upon buyers being legally released from another purchase contract by___date___."

The buyer has now successfully tied up two homes and strengthened their bargaining position by returning to your contract and announcing to you that they have decided against purchasing your property. At this point, most sellers start swearing and making legal threats. Save your breathe. Most attorneys can arrange for any buyer to break a real estate contract if the buyer so desires.

My advice to you is: Let the buyer walk but take the escrow funds, if possible. The reason you should let the buyer walk is simple: Our experience in dealing with thousands of buyers has proven the old real estate adage "Trouble going in, trouble in the end" over and over again. When a Real Estate Agent/Broker starts having problems between the parties at the beginning it will not get better. Never!

Be aware: A buyer who doesn't want your property or who wants to re-negotiate the contract will continue to take you to the wire on every detail. Their knowledge regarding inspectors, appraisals, due dates, loan applications and delays are only a few of the skills buyers bring to the table.

That is why you must demand a high escrow. The higher the escrow, the more control you have. I have seen many a buyer willingly forfeit a $500 or $1,000 escrow. On the other hand, I've seen very few buyers fail to close the transaction when the escrow funds are high.

Two-Step Escrow Suggestion

If the buyer balks at a high escrow, make it a two- or three-step plan:

Step 1) $2,500 escrow now and $2,500 additional escrow after inspections.

Step 2) $5,000 additional escrow—which is non-refundable—after the buyer's loan is approved.

You should take the second step only if there is a long time period between contract date and closing. Usually loan approval is accomplished in 30 to 45 days. If it takes longer, **make all escrow funds non-refundable after the loan is approved** by including the following or similar clause in the contract: "Unless seller cannot provide good title or the property is damaged (i.e., by fire) and cannot be repaired by closing."

REMEMBER: The larger the escrow deposit, the sooner the buyer stops shopping.

CHAPTER ELEVEN

Full Disclosure

Another terrible and costly mistake that homesellers make is **failing to disclose potential future problems or past repairs.**

The age of "buyer beware" in the real estate business has not only expired, but it has been replaced with new laws and court cases where the sellers and Real Estate Agents/Brokers wind up paying for mistakes which could have easily been avoided, sometimes to the tune of three times the amount of damages, plus treble damages and court costs.

Because of a new public awareness about many issues not previously disclosed, the following problems seem to come up most often. This is true even when we include areas of the country where these concerns may or may not exist to any degree which would endanger the new owners:

1) Foundation problems
2) Radon gases
3) Lead-based paint
4) Insecticide spraying or dangerous chemicals
5) Asbestos
6) Chemicals in water sources
7) Neighborhood crime or health problems

In 1986, our firm took the lead in Texas by introducing Sellers Disclosure forms in the greater Austin area. The form consists of two legal-sized pages of questions asking the seller about the history of the home and future potential problems such as zoning changes, neighborhood noises, roadway projects and airplane traffic patterns. We asked questions concerning insect spraying and the types of chemicals used around the home. We asked about underground springs, caverns and the shifting of soil. We asked about fires, electrical and mechanical problems.

Some sellers objected to our intensive quest for anything that we felt could become a future problem. For instance, if a home has had a fire and it has been repaired, most sellers would not be at all happy to disclose this for the obvious fear that it might scare off the buyer. Also undesirable to reveal are electrical problems or the fact that lead-based paint had been used in the house but while there may be a natural reluctance to talk about these things, given our "sue-happy" society, a homeowner better be prepared to answer every possible question up front and before the contract is negotiated and finalized. Some states require the buyers to be furnished a Seller Disclosure before a contractual relationship is complete between the buyer and seller.

In fact, here in Texas, real estate law mandates that a buyer have the option to inspect the property with a fully licensed inspector or engineer.*

* Texas now mandates a Seller Disclosure Statement with the passage of HB 1081 effective January 1, 1994.

In my experience, I've never seen a home that's completely "repair free" and that includes new homes never before occupied. Inspectors are smart enough to know that most homes were built to save the builder money. It's not uncommon to come across an electrical plug which isn't grounded or a glass sliding door that was put in incorrectly.

In many states, sellers who deliberately hide facts about the condition of the home's mechanical features or its state can be sued for up to triple damages, using the Deceptive Trade Practice Act, to recover such damages. This particular law has been singularly responsible for homeowners and Real Estate Agents/Brokers becoming more upfront in disclosing every possible detail about the home.

Why would anyone try to hide conditions that exist in the home? Simple. The main reason is money. It can be expensive to repair heating units, water heaters, dishwashers and other appliances. But it's no longer advisable for a homeowner to try to skirt issues dealing with leaky roofs, plumbing and electrical problems. Buyers want and deserve to know what expenses they will be facing in the near future.

The fastest way to get into potential legal hassles is for the seller to ignore the responsibility of fixing a problem once he or she has knowledge of it.

The majority of all residential areas or subdivisions have neighborhood concerns such as frequent flooding, earthquakes, fires, loud traffic noise, speeding automobiles or barking dogs. In recent years all of our cities have experienced a frightening escalation of crime. Not disclosing these issues where applicable--and any other important information--up front could lead to future legal action by the buyer. When a buyer inquires about crime in the area, refer them to the proper authorities, police and sheriff departments for an accurate picture of the local crime statistics. I don't recommend volunteering information that you do not have first-hand knowledge of. It may result in legal problems, particularly if a serious crime was committed at or near your residence.

The Case of the Haunted House

Recently, there was a nationwide news story about a court case in which the owner had to pay damages, plus court costs, to a buyer who had purchased a residential home that was "haunted." The owner supposedly knew this, but failed to inform the buyer. The buyer discovered the long-kept secret and sued. The jury found the seller guilty and ruled in favor for damages and court costs.

To state it simply, most court cases come down to this: If the buyer had been informed of previous problems, would they have been likely to purchase the property anyway? For instance, if a person was highly allergic to pesticides or chemicals, and the owner either failed to disclose this or was silent when asked about such previous treatment, the law is probably going to rule in favor of the buyer. Had the buyer been informed, then surely the decision to purchase this home would not have been made.

It amounts to the buyer having been lured into making an offer under false pretenses.

The disclosure that we use is divided into ten different sections with each major category requiring detailed information about that section. Often, we ask the same question in several different ways to insure that an owner does not answer the question incorrectly, due to the owner's interpretation of the question. Remember, a disclosure is an effort by the seller to give the buyer accurate information about the property. If the seller chooses to be dishonest about the condition of the property (deliberately misleading the buyer) or if the seller attempts to hide past history or facts, this disclosure could be used by the buyer in a lawsuit, if the buyer claims that the decision to purchase was based on the information in the disclosure.

Here is a partial list of the major issues you should disclose to the buyer. Remember to follow the disclosure laws mandated by your state.

1) Homeowners Association
2) Warranties
3) Features and Equipment: What conveys?
4) Property History: Including neighborhood conditions, zoning, and future use
5) Water/Waste Water
6) Utilities
7) Security Systems
8) Environmental Issues
9) Structural Information

10)   Taxes·

If your Real Estate Agent/Broker does not have a disclosure form for you to use, you may choose to order our three page legal-size disclosure form that asks 190 questions pertaining to the property. Please see order blank in the back of the book.

CHAPTER TWELVE

Looking Your Best

Unless you're selling a fixer-upper, then you must do the fixing-up before you sell. Your home must look its very best when it goes on the market.

Remember: You never get a second chance to make a first impression.

There are two types of homes in every marketplace.
1) The home we live in on a daily basis.
2) The home we make ready for sale and present to the public.

Let's face it: it may take some hard work to get your home ready for prospective buyers to look at, but whatever steps you take to increase the chances of your home selling quickly will ease the frustration and inconvenience to you and your family during the process of having total strangers looking at your home.

Some real estate companies offer booklets and handouts to help you "present" your home for sale. The most impressive video I've seen on the subject is produced by Better Homes and Gardens. It is called "Home Merchandising." Please see information in the back of this book for ordering the videotape. It is a 45-minute video which takes you through each room in your home and gives you detailed instructions on how to arrange furniture, how to organize your kitchen and how to make your home seem larger and more spacious. Cleaning up clutter and disposing of unnecessary furniture will help present your home in the best possible (and positive) light.

There are at least two major mistakes which homeowners overlook regarding the look of their home and the impression it makes.

1) They never really look at their home through the prospective buyer's eyes.
2) Sellers seldom realize some buyers will be driving neighborhoods and will make a snap decision to either call about the home or pass it by based upon their impression of your home from the street. If it is land-scaped and attractive (without clutter in the yard), you improve your chances considerably.

What the Buyer Usually Sees

Take a drive through any neighborhood on the weekend and you will see some of the exterior "mistakes" of homes that are for sale. The following bad impressions they make will deter a prospective buyer from calling the Real Estate Agent/Broker:

1) Garage doors completely open and showing a messy garage.

2) Cars parked in driveway and in front of house.
3) Repair work being done on cars in driveway.
4) Bicycles, lawnmowers and lawn equipment scattered about the yard.
5) Boats or campers parked in driveway.
6) Immobilized cars on jacks.
7) Car being worked on or waxed in the drive way.

REMEMBER: On the weekend, buyers drive through areas and neighborhoods they want to live in.

What happens to most homes on the weekend, especially if there are teenagers in the household, is that it becomes a beehive of activity. And that "activity" can look very messy from a buyer's point of view.

Cars parked in the driveway hide the view of the home and they take attention away from the exterior. Open garage doors expose not only the contents of the garage but if the garage is cluttered with boxes, etc., buyers immediately assume that the home has little or no storage space.

The more attractive your home shows from the street, the more likely it will sell quickly, particularly if the price is competitive.

According to the National Association of Real Estate Agents/Brokers, 17% of inbound calls to a real estate firm are from yard signs. Buyers have already seen the home from the outside and are impressed enough to call for the price, size and other relevant information.

Weekends should be fun, but please make sure that they are not costing you a potential sale because the prospective buyer's first impression is a bad one.

How To See Your Home Through a Buyer's Eyes:

Step across the street from your home and take a few minutes to really inspect the exterior and the property, including the landscaping. What do you see? Here is a checklist of items for the exterior of your home.

The overall appearance is:
great _____   good _____   poor _____

Is the lawn trimmed and neat?
yes _____   no _____

Is the grass edged?
yes _____   no _____

Are the bushes trimmed and neat?
yes _____   no _____

Are there plants, such as blooming flowers?
yes _____   no _____

Is the porch/doorway inviting? Clean?

        yes _____   no _____

Are windows clean and in good repair?

        yes _____   no _____

Is the garage door down?

        yes _____   no _____

Is the garage clean?

        yes _____   no _____

Are rain gutters clean?

        yes _____   no _____

Is paint fresh and free of peeling?

        yes _____   no _____

Are window screens repaired and free of tears?

        yes _____   no _____

Are garden hoses picked up?

        yes _____   no _____

Are boats, RV's, miscellaneous items stored?

        yes _____   no _____

Is the roof in good shape?

        yes _____   no _____

Is exterior lighting in proper working condition?

     yes _____   no _____

Are house numbers fixed and easily read?

     yes _____   no _____

Are drapes, blinds and exterior shutters uniform from street view?

     yes _____   no _____

Are trees trimmed to prevent limbs touching the home?

     yes _____   no _____

The following checklist is for the interior of your home when a prospective buyer walks through it.

Are carpets clean and free of worn areas?

     yes _____   no _____

Are interior lights in proper working condition?

     yes _____   no _____

Are drapes or blinds open to help the home show as much light as possible?

     yes _____   no _____

Are pets outdoors? (They should be.)

yes _____   no _____

Are all kitchen counter tops neat and tidy?
Remove all items from counter top (i.e., toasters, electric can openers.)

yes _____   no _____

Have you taken all notes, magnets, etc., off of refrigerator doors?

yes _____   no _____

Are all AC/Heating filters clean?

yes _____   no _____

Are the ceiling fans clean, especially the blades?

yes _____   no _____

If someone in your home is a smoker, try professional odor removers. Large janitorial supply houses or vacuum cleaner stores usually carry these items, and they are very effective in destroying odors, not masking them with another scent.

Are your closets organized?

yes _____   no _____

Are unnecessary items boxed and stored?

        yes _____   no _____

Has unnecessary furniture been removed?

        yes _____   no _____

The interior should be painted in light colors such as white or off white. Use a semi-gloss latex paint, which enables future cleaning with a wet towel and soap. Flat latex paint does not clean easily.

Additional tips:

When the home is being shown:

1) Leave, unless you've been asked to stay.
2) Turn on soft classical music.
3) Leave lights on to improve showing.
4) Flowers make an impression. Use them in dining and living areas.
5) Leave telephone answering machine on, voice control completely turned down, and set it to catch first ring (a ringing telephone will annoy buyers).

As I've said earlier, all this may mean a lot of extra time and effort for you, but won't it be worth it when your home sells quickly?

CHAPTER THIRTEEN

Mortgage Lenders and Other Practical Advice

Some loan agreements still contain language which penalizes the homeowner for 30 days worth of additional interest if the mortgage company was not notified about the potential sale. To avoid this "highway robbery" charge, you should do the following:

1) Notify the mortgage company 30 days in advance by certified or registered letter or overnight delivery service. Request a return receipt.
2) Keep the receipt in your file.
3) Every time you make a payment include a note of your intent to sell. Keep a copy and a record of the mailing date.
4) Ask the mortgage company for a written response to your notification.
5) Ask your mortgage company for a written verification of the loan balance on your property, including any interest due to the day of closing.

Offer a Home Warranty!

Most home warranty programs cover the homeowner during the listing period for mechanical problems with the dishwasher, garbage disposal, electrical heating and cooling units for a small fee. Inground pools, spas and hot tubs sometimes carry additional premiums, but they too can be covered.

Some companies now require a pre-inspection of items which the homeowner wants covered. If all the mechanical items are working, the insurance warranty program is issued without exceptions.

Such a home warranty program not only benefits the seller but it impresses the buyer, who's relieved that his or her liability during the next year will be limited to the deductible amount which varies from $35 to $100 per service call depending on the warranty company.

The Loan Process

Major problems often develop during the loan process. Therefore, it's up to you and your agent to monitor that process without violating the privacy act. **You have the right to monitor, but not inquire, as to exact financial details of any problems.** For instance, if a student loan is outstanding, the seller is allowed to know that the loan is the reason why the buyer may not qualify but not the extent of the past due amount or monies owed on the loan.

Finding out two days prior to your closing that the buyer or mortgage company let the ball drop somewhere during the loan process will tend to create all kinds of problems, especially if your moving plans are contingent upon the buyer's closing your transaction.

There are different types of financial institutions which lend money to purchase real estate. The most common are:

> Mortgage Companies
> Savings and Loan Associations
> Banks
> Credit Unions
> Private Investors

Important: Consumers normally are not aware that mortgage bankers and mortgage brokers are not the same. A mortgage banker actually is the company which has lined up established investors who are willing to lend money for real property, provided that the buyers meet certain guidelines established by Fannie Mae and Freddie Mac. These investors also have stipulated the type of properties they are willing to loan money on, for how long and the amount of return they want on their investment.

A mortgage broker is an individual who "brokers" loans to the mortgage banker The broker arranges to take the loan application and provide support documents and other required forms to the mortgage banker so the loan can be approved. It is important to understand the process in order for you to monitor the loan.

How to Monitor the Loan Process:

1) Never rely on verbal communication. Ask for and demand a fax or written communication update. If an agent or mortgage company will not provide a written progress report, **WATCH OUT!!**

2) Ask for a weekly update of the loan process.

3) Ask for immediate notification if a problem arises with the loan along with an assessment if the issue can be resolved.

At this point you need to be clear about the role the underwriter will play in this process. The underwriter has the power to approve, disapprove or question any item in the package, including the appraised value.

Do not rely upon the loan officer's opinion, ask for the underwriter's opinion about the problem, because this person will make the judgement call weeks down the line anyway. If the underwriter doesn't approve of the situation then the loan will be denied.

Initiate Title Search Immediately

Ask your title company to open title to insure there are no problems which would keep you from passing clear title to the property. The reason you check on title now is to avoid problems at closing. (Most state laws require that the buyer have time to examine the title policy and to object to title exceptions.)

The Best Tips to Save You Money and Headaches
(Not intended to be legal advice)

Once you are successful in negotiating a contract on your home, it is quite common to start the process of vacating the property. Be sure to use the following tips before you commit to a new home or lease.

1) Make sure any contract you sign has clear language and provisions while spelling out that "this contract is contingent upon the sale, closing and funding" of your property on or before a certain date.

2) Ask for additional language which specifies that your full earnest money or escrow funds will be refunded without deductions.

3) Ask your attorney to inspect and advise you of any legal or financial considerations which you may have missed in your haste.

4) Make sure your moving company's contract has a provision and right for you to cancel if the sale of your property does not close.

How the Contract/Loan Process Works:

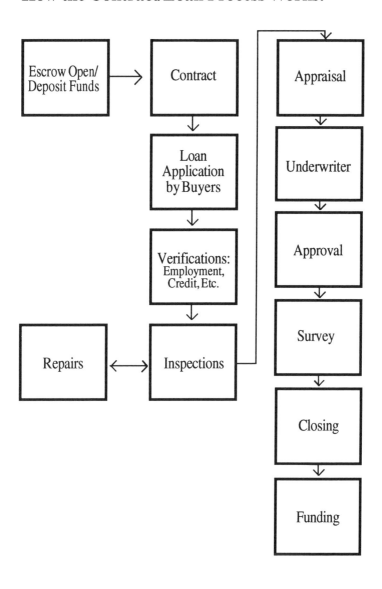

Last Minute Tips for a Smooth Closing, or The Little Things We Fail to Do!

1) **Settle the Repair Issues.** Prior to closing, arrange with the buyer's Agent/Broker to settle any issues about repairs or other contractual obligations. If repairs are being handled by the seller, I recommend that the buyer provide a priority list of items in writing so everyone understands exactly who is responsible for the repairs. If the buyer has agreed to the repairs, be sure that some type of written agreement spells out which repairs are being paid for by the seller. If the repairs are minor, usually the Agent/Broker can write up a general agreement of understanding (unless prohibited by law); otherwise, either the title company or your attorney should draw up this agreement. Be sure to include language stating that the seller is not responsible for future repairs or discovery of additional issues not addressed in this agreement.

2) **Your mortgage interest is paid in arrears!** When you make your monthly house payment on the first of the month, the interest due is for the previous month. Depending on the day of closing, you will owe for the number of days you maintained ownership of the property. Expect the payoff of your loan to be higher

than your present loan amount because the mortgage company will include the interest due up to the date of closing.

3) **Taxes are due at closing!** Remember, your taxes are due up to the last day you own the property. If more taxes are due at the end of the year, most buyers have the right to ask you to pay your share of the increased amount. Example: If your taxes were increased $600 for the year and you owned the property for six months, the new owners are due an additional $300 at the end of the year for the period of time you actually owned the property.

4) **Leave your home clean.** Leaving your home in move-in condition creates less of a problem with the smaller issues in the months after a closing. Most buyers want to feel they made a good choice and a good buy in selecting your home, but if the house is a mess when they arrive to move in, and then later, a few minor problems surface, guess who's going to be blamed? If a major problem develops after closing and your relationship is already distressed because the move-in condition of the house was a disappointment, your buyer may seek legal action much more quickly than if you had left the property in very satisfactory condition. The Golden Rule really plays an important role here.

5)   **A tip for the wise!** Tell your neighbors, family and friends exacly where you have moved and the new telephone numbers. During the big move and all of the confusion, it is easy to leave something behind or someone might need to be in touch due to an emergency. It is very common for pets to wander back to their old neighborhood.

Other Practical Advice and Tips

When Things Go Wrong

It's impossible for everything to go smoothly during the sale of your home. **Something** is bound to go wrong. After all, you're only human. Therefore, having a back-up plan is one of the most important factors in recovering quickly to insure that your home is available to the buyers who are currently in the marketplace.

For example, if you've signed a contract with a buyer and the loan process is starting to develop some glitches, it's imperative that some of your energy --and that of your Agent/Broker--become focused on a two-part plan. Plan A is to scc if the buyer's loan problem can be solved in time to meet the closing date. Plan B is to start drafting a new marketing plan in case the house has to be put back on the market. Advertising, including marketing to other Agents/Brokers, and an open house will help attract attention quickly, which is what you need.

If the house is put back on the market, ask your Agent/Broker to withdraw the listing from the current multiple listing service and place your home all over again as a new listing. This procedure usually gives your listing a new, higher-sequenced number with the multiple listing service. Having a new number helps to guard against the impression that the home has been on the market for a long time.

Escrow Funds Are Not Refunded At Closing
A vast majority of mortgage companies refund your escrow monies for taxes and insurance only after your loan has been paid off. Each month you pay 1/12th or more of your taxes and insurance into an escrow fund in order for the mortgage company to pay the taxes and premiums as they come due. After payoff, a separate check is mailed to you closing your balance in the fund. This normally does not appear anywhere on your closing statement.

A FINAL WORD

Nothing tugs at our heartstrings in quite the same way as moving or planning to move from our home. Nothing else we ever buy or sell is quite so intimate. We're often torn between wanting to hang on to the past memories and looking forward to a new place, a new city, a new environment--in short, the future. But it's our present home that contains all the goals and hopes, the hurts and disappointments that we've accumulated over the years. When the process of moving disturbs these memories, all sorts of emotions begin to surface. This emotional and sentimental attachment to our home must be balanced by the disciplined, business-like approach that's absolutely necessary when we ready our home for sale.

Planning your move will be much easier if you can avoid making the mistakes that create additional anxiety during the selling process. I have given you an excellent road map with which to travel from the moment you decide to sell to writing the contract for the sale of your home.

It's imperative that you start the selling process with a clear goal of why you want to sell and that you each an agreement with all parties who share your home on the necessity to move. Making every member of your family a part of the process will enable your home to sell more quickly because everyone can--and should--share in the fixing and cleaning-up campaign to ready your home to show.

Selling a home today is more complicated than ever before due to increasing and changing rules, regulations and mandated seller's disclosure laws. If you choose a real estate professional to help you, make sure you use the simple guidelines I've provided in Chapter 11.

Pricing your home properly is the number one factor which determines success or failure. Trying to "test" the market or leaving room to negotiate is a sure-fire way to end up with your home sitting on the market forever.

Buyers always determine and drive the real estate market, regardless of a hot or declining market trend. It is the buyer's willingness to purchase that determines your home's value. Setting an inflated price prevents some buyers from ever **seeing** your home.

Follow the simple tips I've given you when interviewing a Real Estate Agent/Broker. Make sure you obtain a marketing plan that includes advertising. While it's important to have all agreements spelled out prior to listing your home, it's also essential that you agree to have your home in market condition throughout this process.

Selling your home should be a fun, enjoyable experience. Avoiding the mistakes that so many sellers make will help you remove the obstacles that, all too often, make the procedure unpleasant and unnecessarily difficult.

The greatest compliment that I can be paid is having a home seller say to me, "Gosh, it was so easy." Then I know I've done my job well, and everyone's satisfied. I want you to have this kind of experience-- that's the purpose of my book. Good Luck!

AVOID THE PITFALLS THAT COST HOME BUYERS AND SELLERS BIG MONEY!

Special Booklet Reports! Now you can obtain special coaching by Bob Easter. Detailed instructions to help you learn the ropes of home buying or selling. Take advantage of these step-by-step resources that will put you in control when you plan to buy or sell real estate.

Your Guarantee. You cannot lose! I personally guarantee your satisfaction. My reputation for helping the consumer understand the process of buying and selling real estate is very important to me. Order any special report and look it over. If it is not exactly what you want, you may return it for a full refund at any time, for any reason.

Bob Easter

HELPFUL HOME BUYING REPORTS

#2210
Before you are sued, learn how to avoid lawsuits. Tell the buyer everything about your property including past, present, and future problems or conditions. Over 190 questions to answer about your home. This 3-page legal size disclosure form includes such rare items as haunted houses, buried ammunition, future airports, and crime rates. Save thousands of dollars by disclosing more than is required. Order now, before you show and sell! $9.95

#2375
Appraisal problems could side-track your contract even when the buyers are willing to pay your asking price. Learn how to help the appraiser see the value of your property. This checklist of items could save you headaches and a lot of money. Don't blame the appraiser when you could have avoided this problem by ordering our "Appraiser Tips" booklet. $3.95

#2409
How to ask the right questions to stop a Real Estate Agent from taking advantage of your inexperience. Know the ropes before you start the interviewing process. My checklist will force the agent to be upfront and honest about what you can expect for your money. Interview with complete confidence. This list is a must! $3.95

#2517
Expose your home! Sell it quick! The perfect marketing plan to keep your home in front of active, productive Real Estate Agents/ Brokers and serious buyers. Along with a detailed 30-day calendar to keep your agent on top of the other listings in your city. Here is the secret to marketing. $6.00

#2534
Buyer eyes never lie! See what the buyers focus on when previewing your home. The little things will cost you a contract! The time to fix up is before the buyer views your home. $4.95

#3111
"10 Money Saving Tips Before You Sell Your Home". A favorite booklet lets you in on 10 action steps to take before you see the first buyers. If you miss this booklet, you could miss a sale. $3.00

#4310
Stop throwing money away. Read my "10 Money Saving Tips Before You Buy a Home". Learn precisely what you must do to protect your interest when buying a home. Packed full of expert advice to keep you from making major mistakes. $3.00

#2562
What every home buyer absolutely must demand before looking for a home. Be protected prior to looking for a home or submitting a contract. This crucial interview process leaves no room for any Agent to avoid representing your interest in a real estate transaction. This report provides you the steps to saving thousands of dollars and keeps you from overpaying for property. Order Now! $6.00

#2609
Distinguishing facts from fiction. Proven techniques to show you how to understand what is important to the buyer or seller. When emotions run high, learn to settle issues quickly before the little things cause a party to quit negotiating before all parties agree. $4.00

#2642
How to sell your home from an open house. Proven step-by-step detailed planning that works! No one else has the proven success formula for open houses. Selling your home from one open house could be a very real possibility if you follow the step-by-step plans. Easy to read and understand, this one report could fill up your home with buyers who are interested in purchasing today. $12.00

SPECIAL OFFER -
Save over 30%!
Order all of these crucial reports for $39.00. The regular price is $56.80, but you can have all of the reports for only $39.00 Save $17.80 by ordering all the reports now! Add $3.50 for shipping and handling.

HELPFUL HOME BUYING VIDEOS

#2709 - Video
Avoid obstacles sellers often overlook. This 45-minute video produced by Better Homes and Gardens guides you step-by-step, room-by-room to prepare your home to sell. Learn how to concentrate your efforts on key areas from the buyers perspective. A must see if you are serious about selling. $19.95

#2813 - Video
Buying a home is a complex project! Knowing what your needs are and how much house you can afford will improve your confidence to buy. This video explains why it is critical to select the right Agent to help you negotiate the best deal for you. Home shopping without this video could cost you thousands of dollars. $19.95

#2971 - Video
The most important decision is pricing your home to sell. Buyers are comparison shoppers. Having a negotiation cushion could cost you, especially if the buyers never see your home because of the price. Overlook this video and you will lose money quickly by pricing your home out of the market. $19.95

For ordering information see next page!

ORDER FORM

Telephone Orders:
Call **toll free** 1(800) 848-5593.
Have your credit card ready.
For faster service, fill out order
blank first.

Fax Orders:
(512) 346-2272. Send order blank.

Postal Orders:
Easter and Easter, Inc.
4212 Lostridge Drive, Suite 200
Austin, Texas 78731, USA Tel:
(512) 483-7432

Please send the following *Helpful Home Buying Reports*:

- ❑ #2210 - $9.95
- ❑ #2375 - $3.95
- ❑ #2409 - $3.95
- ❑ #2517 - $6.00
- ❑ #2534 - $4.95

- ❑ #3111 - $3.00
- ❑ #4310 - $3.00
- ❑ #2562 - $6.00
- ❑ #2609 - $4.00
- ❑ #2642 - $12.00

Please send the following
Money Saving Videos:

- ❑ #2709 - $19.95
- ❑ #2813 - $19.95
- ❑ #2971 - $19.95

SPECIAL OFFER
Save 30%!
- ❑ All Reports - $39.00
Regularly $56.80
Does not include Videos or shipping and handling.

Ship to:

Company: _____

Name: _____

Address: _____

City: _____ State: _____ Zip: _____

Telephone: (____) _____

Payment:

❑ Checks   Make payable to: Easter and Easter, Inc.
(Foreign orders, please use credit card, send check drawn on a U.S. bank or send an international money order.)

❑ Credit Card   ❑ Visa   ❑ MasterCard   ❑ American Express

Card Number: _____ Exp. Date: _____

Cardholder Name: _____ Signature: _____
Prices subject to change without notice. Quantity prices available on request.

Shipping: **U.S.:** $2.00 for the first report or video and .75 for each additional one, or
$3.50 each for Air Mail. Your order is normally shipped within 24 hours. Books are usually
shipped via the Postal Service's *Book Rate* which takes four days to three weeks in the U.S.
On request, we will ship UPS, overnight delivery or truck.